# My
# MIGHTY
# JOURNEY

For those who came before

those now

and those to come

# My MIGHTY JOURNEY

## A Waterfall's Story

**John Coy**

Illustrations by **Gaylord Schanilec**

Minnesota Historical Society Press

I am
a **POWERFUL**

WATERFALL.

I listen.
I pay attention.
I have a long memory.

You might find it hard to believe
but I have moved through time.

I remember
twelve thousand years ago.
Water **ROARS** over my

MASSIVE

FACE

wearing away
my sandstone
body.
My limestone ledges jut out
and when these
crack
and crash
below
my new stone face emerges
upriver
from the
fallen
rock.

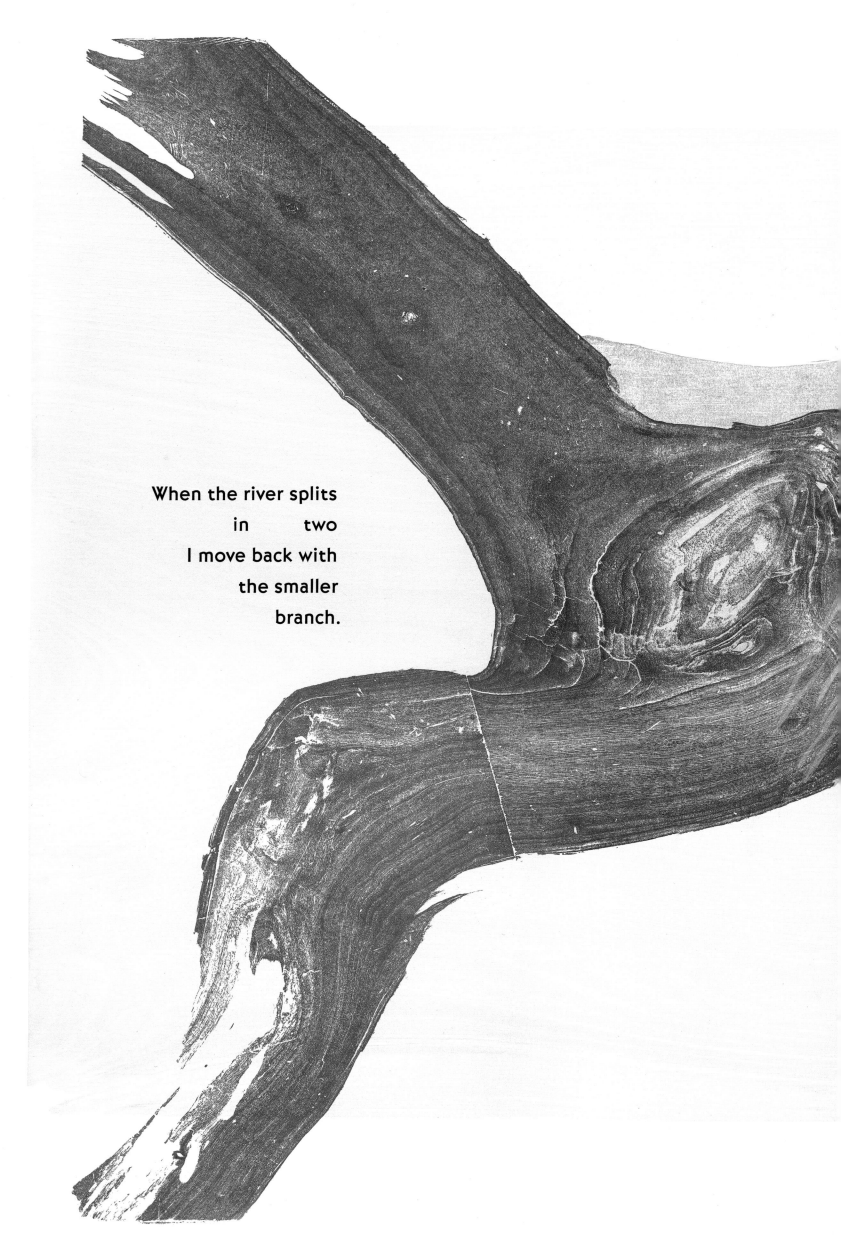

When the river splits
in     two
I move back with
the smaller
branch.

Nearby, men throw spears
into the belly of a

# WOOLLY MAMMOTH.

They give thanks to the animal
because they're desperate for food.

Where a creek joins the river
ice hangs
off
my face
like a
beard.

People sit around a fire telling
**stories about me**.

Off my shoulder
a pack of

# WOLVES

silhouetted in
the moonlight
searches for
something
to eat.

As I move up the narrow gorge
                    I become smaller.
A boy and his grandfather
catch **FISH** below me.

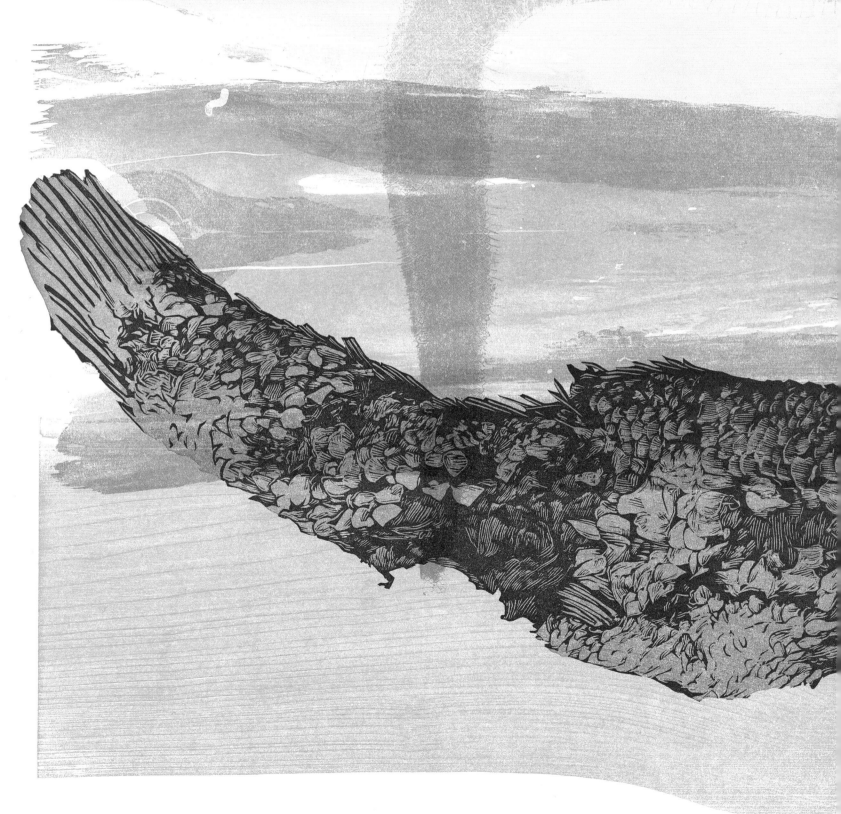

The **GRANDFATHER**
describes how I've changed
so that the **BOY** will be able
to tell his **GRANDCHILDREN**.

When an island is in the middle of me
a Dakota man who calls me **OWAMNIYOMNI**
offers a decorated beaver robe
and asks for blessings.

On the bank, a Franciscan priest
claims he's discovered me
and says my name is le Saut Saint Antoine de Padouë
the **FALLS OF SAINT ANTHONY** of Padua.

When I recede again
a mother and daughter taste chokecherries
and decide the fruit's not quite ripe.

Back in their garden
they check corn and beans and squash.
The girl looks up at me, then

WATERS

thirsty plants.

Survey'd by Cap.t Carver, Nov. 17. 1766.

The falls of S.t Anthony in the River MISSISSIPPI,
near 2400 Miles from its entrance into the Gulf of Mexico.

M. A. Rooker sculp.

Haight of the Fall
30 feet Perpend.r

Broadth near
600 feet.

People pour in and scramble to harness

MY POWER.

Belts hum blades spin and metal **CLaNKs** as white pine is cut into lumber.

When booms break logs escape **CRASHING** over my face and jamming in front of me.

As I move farther upriver
workers begin a tunnel
from one island
to another

BUT DISASTER STRIKES.

The tunnel

COLLAPSES and a whirlpool

sucks debris
and blasts it out
the other end.

# "THE FALLS IS GOING OUT!"

a boy yells.

I'm terrified that this is the end.

The break **E X P A N D S** and I **panic.**

Finally, men build dams and fill the tunnel. Later, they put up a cement wall and construct a WOODEN APRON on top of me.

I am cramped and cannot see but it's the only way to save me.

After my long journey I'm locked in place.

It is painful to be confined while so much changes nearby.

TRAINS OF WHEAT ROLL IN.

UP
GOES

the **LARGEST**
flour mill
ever built.

Passengers cross the

STONE ARCH BRIDGE

and call out when they see me.

Minneapolis uses my power and boasts of making the

BEST & MOST

flour in the world.

But as electricity
replaces
my waterpower

mills in the area
shut down.

Workers
create
a huge

# LOCK

to move boats
and barges
around me.

An observation deck opens
and a girl admires
my new concrete cover.
But barge traffic
is less than planned and
business near me declines.

Abandoned buildings crumble. The last train crosses the bridge and men put up a fence to keep trespassers off.

**FIRE** breaks out in an old mill and blazes in the night.

Far fewer visitors find me.

**TODAY**
the Stone Arch Bridge is open to walkers, runners, and bikers.

Once again, PEOPLE come to me.

Nearby, Dakota drummers **POUND OUT BEATS** and sing the old songs. Former mills have been converted into places to live and work.

After my

# MIGHTY JOURNEY

fifteen miles over
twelve thousand years
I stay in this spot.

I am no longer as **MASSIVE** as I was.
I don't receive as many offerings.
But I am still powerful.

I am still here.

# More About My Mighty Journey

### PORTRAIT

The waterfall at the heart of Minneapolis existed fifteen miles downriver twelve thousand years ago—where downtown St. Paul is now. Over half a mile wide, it was bigger than Niagara Falls is today. An enormous volume of water flowing from melting glaciers caused it to erode upriver.

### EROSION

Limestone is harder than sandstone, so falling water eroded the sandstone base, leaving protruding limestone ledges. When these cracked and crashed, the waterfall moved back, displaying a new stone face. Then the process began all over again. The waterfall left behind chunks of limestone in the river that showed its path.

### CONFLUENCE

The area where today's Minnesota and Mississippi Rivers meet, Bdote Mni Sota, is extremely important to Dakota people. For more than twelve thousand years, humans have lived here. When the waterfall was nearby, they hunted giant beavers, mastodons, and woolly mammoths.

### FIRE & ICE

The waterfall moved up the Mississippi gorge, but as less water flowed, its erosion slowed. The "creek" is today's Minnehaha Creek, and nearby Minnehaha Falls provides another example of water flowing over limestone on top of sandstone. This smaller waterfall has also moved as it has eroded.

### DOGFISH

For people who lived near the river, fish were an important source of food. One way to catch them was by using copper hooks, like this one that is more than two thousand years old. Even though the waterfall was smaller, it continued to erode so that a grandfather could show his grandchild how it had changed.

### ISLAND

In some spots, the strong stone didn't erode, leaving islands in the waterfall. On one of these, later called Spirit Island, Father Louis Hennepin claimed he saw a Dakota man make an offering of a beaver robe in October 1680. Dakota and Ojibwe people described the falls differently, but Hennepin named it after his patron saint.

### THREE SISTERS

In addition to hunting and fishing, Indigenous people grew corn, beans, squash, and other vegetables and collected plants, nuts, berries, wild rice, and maple syrup. In 1766, Jonathan Carver visited the area and drew a picture of the falls. He wrote: "a more pleasing and picturesque view, I believe, can not be found throughout the universe."

### MNI SOTA

An image of Bdote Mni Sota, where the waters are so clear they reflect the clouds. After thousands of years of people living along the river, the waterfall and its surroundings will soon change dramatically because of new people moving in.

### SAWMILLS

The waterpower of the falls generated much discussion. In 1848, Franklin Steele constructed a dam and sawmill on the east bank of the river. Over the next sixty years, the vast forests of Minnesota were cut down and logs floated downriver to supply the growing demands of farms, towns, and cities.

### COLLAPSE

In 1868, William Eastman and John Merriam began a tunnel from Hennepin Island to Nicollet Island to increase waterpower. On October 4, 1869, water poured into the tunnel, and the next morning it collapsed. Volunteers plugged the hole with dirt, rocks, and mattresses, but nothing held. People feared the entire falls would be destroyed.

### APRON

Multiple attempts failed to stabilize the area until men built a 1,850-foot cement wall across the river in 1876. This dike was supposed to last for one hundred years, and that date is long past. Later, a wooden apron covered the face of the falls to prevent erosion and hold it in place.

### FLOUR MILLS

In 1880, the Washburn A Mill became the world's largest flour mill. A year later it lost that title to the Pillsbury A Mill across the river. These mills helped Minneapolis lead the world in flour production for the next fifty years. The Stone Arch Bridge opened in 1883, providing rail passengers a dramatic view of the mills and the falls.

### LOCK & DAM

After the use of steam power and electricity became common, flour mills no longer needed the falls' waterpower and smaller mills developed elsewhere. Two arches of the Stone Arch Bridge were removed for the large-scale construction of Upper St. Anthony Lock and Dam, which opened in 1963.

### FIRE!

In 1978, the final passenger train crossed the Stone Arch Bridge as more mills in the area shut down. On February 26, 1991, a fire broke out in one of these abandoned mills, the Washburn A Mill. The fire lit up the riverbank on a cold night before it was finally extinguished.

### TODAY

The Stone Arch Bridge reopened in 1994, and the ruins of the Washburn A Mill became the site of the Mill City Museum in 2003. Many old mills, including the Pillsbury A Mill, are now studios, offices, and condos. Each July, the Owámni Falling Water Festival, featuring Indigenous food, art, drumming, and singing, takes place near the falls.

### PANORAMA

Owamniyomni, the Falls of St. Anthony, is the only major waterfall on the Mississippi River. Come visit this significant place and share the story. What do you think will happen here next?

# Author & Illustrator Note

*My Mighty Journey* is the biggest book collaboration either of us has ever undertaken. Unlike the process of most picture books in which writer and artist create separately, we have shared ideas on text, images, and layout for years. From the start, we planned two different editions: a fine press version and this trade one.

We began our work by taking long walks along the Mississippi River, tracing the path the waterfall traveled. We looked at plants, trees, rocks, water, and animals at different times of the year. We also made sure to talk with people who knew more about the original inhabitants, the river, and the land than we did.

Our collaboration expanded to include book artists Paul Nylander, Barbara Eijadi, Sorcha Douglas, and Hans Koch. Many interns and volunteers were also essential, including Emily Pressprich, Greta Lapcinski, Paris Fobbe, Rayan Macalin, Kerri Mulcare, Ellen Janda, Matthew Zimmerman, Rebecca Staley, and Monica Edwards Larson.

From the beginning, we wanted the art to reflect the nature of the river and waterfall. Multiple times group members walked the banks of the river and collected bark, wood, and roots of fallen trees, along with limestone, bricks, a snake skin, and even a dead dogfish. These materials were then used to create the images in the book.

The biggest influence on the words and art, however, came through our conversations with Diane Wilson, Ernie Whiteman, and everyone at Dream of Wild Health, a Native-owned farm that grows indigenous plants to connect people with traditional foods. Diane and Ernie generously guided us to a deeper understanding of this place where people have lived for more than twelve thousand years. Recognizing that it's less than three percent of that time since Europeans arrived is a reminder of how many of us are newcomers and how much

we have to learn from the people who have been here so long. We are also grateful to the team at Dream of Wild Health for sharing the important plants that are the basis for the images of growth and cultivation in the book.

In addition, we relied on the guidance of historian David Wiggins, who conducted tours at the falls for many years with the Minnesota Historical Society and the National Park Service. David's help

and suggestions were invaluable. Patricia Emerson, head of archaeology at the Minnesota Historical Society, shared the collection of spear points that go back thousands of years. She also emphasized the importance of copper tools to Indigenous people and showed us the beautiful fishhook that is pictured in the book. Jim Rock, planetarium program director at the University of Minnesota Duluth, was particularly helpful in sharing his knowledge about time, the falls, and Dakota cosmology.

The original images in this book were created at Minnesota Center for Book Arts in Minneapolis. We are grateful to the artists there for their enthusiasm and encouragement.

Editor Shannon Pennefeather, production manager Dan Leary, curator of art Brian Szott, intern Lisa Finander, and the staff at Minnesota Historical Society Press supported this project in so many ways, even allowing us the unusual freedom of working for years without a deadline as we realized how much we had to learn. For this and for all of those who helped make *My Mighty Journey* possible, we are grateful.

And over and over, we give thanks to the waterfall.

# Selected Bibliography

Anfinson, John. *River of History: A Historic Resources Study of the Mississippi National River and Recreation Area.* St. Paul, MN: US Army Corps of Engineers, 2003.

Anfinson, Scott F. "Archaeology at the Riverside: Unearthing the Invisible." *Minnesota History* 58, no. 5–6 (2003): 321–31.

Kane, Lucille M. *The Falls of St. Anthony: The Waterfall That Built Minneapolis.* St. Paul: Minnesota Historical Society Press, 1996.

Long Soldier, Layli. *Whereas.* Minneapolis, MN: Graywolf Press, 2017.

Pennefeather, Shannon M., ed. *Mill City: A Visual History of the Minneapolis Mill District.* St. Paul: Minnesota Historical Society Press, 2003.

Sherman, Sean, with Beth Dooley. *The Sioux Chef's Indigenous Kitchen.* Minneapolis: University of Minnesota Press, 2017.

Westerman, Gwen, and Bruce White. *Mni Sota Makoce: The Land of the Dakota.* St. Paul: Minnesota Historical Society Press, 2012.

Wilson, Diane. *Beloved Child: A Dakota Way of Life.* St. Paul, MN: Borealis Books, 2011.

For more information about the creation of the images, check out the project blog at **MyMightyJourney.tumblr.com**.

A portion of the royalties from this book will benefit Dream of Wild Health, a Native-owned and -run farm that grows indigenous plants and connects people with traditional foods.

mnhspress.org

The Minnesota Historical Society Press is a member of the Association of University Presses.

Manufactured in Canada.

10 9 8 7 6 5 4 3 2 1

♾ The paper used in this publication meets the minimum requirements of the American National Standard for Information Sciences—Permanence for Printed Library Materials, ANSI Z39.48-1984.

International Standard Book Number
ISBN: 978-1-68134-008-1 (hardcover)

Library of Congress Cataloging-in-Publication Data available upon request.

*My Mighty Journey* was designed and set in type by Paul Nylander at illustrada design, Minneapolis. The typefaces are URW Bernhard Gothic, based on the 1930 ATF Lucian Bernhard typeface, and Fairplex by Zuzana Licko of Emigre.